BodySense

A WOMAN'S 5-STEP BODY GUIDE

Understand what your body is telling you to alleviate pain, make better decisions at work, and deepen relationships.

Heidi A. Sauder, Ph.D.

David R. Hubbard, MD

Leanna R. Fredrich, Life Coach

Initial Printing 07/2010

TABLE OF CONTENTS

FORWARD

When we began treating headache in our clinic twenty-five years ago, Dave Hubbard, our colleagues, and I made some fascinating discoveries about our patients that were critical for teaching us how to help them to alleviate their pain and improve the quality of their lives (as well as our own!). The first and most important thing we learned was that our patients had surprisingly little awareness of some of their most valuable bodily sensations. Tension headache patients could not feel the sensations of muscle tension that could have told them in advance that their next headache was building and given them the opportunity to respond early and stop the pain before it began. Migraine patients were unable to feel the sensations of blood vessel constriction that would have given them advance warning of an impending headache allowing them time to act to head off the painful and debilitating symptoms.

We discovered that we could teach our patients to learn to feel these sensations, to identify the situations that caused these sensations, and to take action to stop the development of the pain. Our patients were usually surprised to discover that the situations that triggered feelings of muscle tension and blood vessel constriction were primarily emotional ones. When we studied the kinds of emotions that triggered tension and migraine headaches we realized that they were different for each type of headache. The kinds of situations that triggered sensations of muscle tension in our tension headache patients were ones that most people would describe as frustrating, irritating, annoying, or anger-provoking. The situations that triggered sensations of vascular constriction in our migraine patients were ones that most people would describe as fearful or anxiety-provoking.

We came to realize that our headache patients were unaware of the feelings of anger and fear in their bodies. They also didn't know what situations were triggering these feelings that they weren't feeling and what to do to resolve the feelings. And we discovered that when the feelings were unresolved, the muscle tension, or vascular constriction that caused these feelings persisted and led to the headache pain.

We were intrigued by these connections between changes in the body's physiology (in the case of headache - muscle tension and vascular constriction) emotions, and pain. We wondered if people could be unaware of other body sensations and emotions. We also wondered if being unaware of other kinds of feelings could lead to different types of pain or other medical symptoms. And we wondered if being unaware of important feelings could lead to psychological or relationship problems, and have negative effects on the individual's quality of life and happiness.

Further clinical work and study led us to conclude that the answer to all of these questions was, yes. We then began to wonder how people could come to be unaware of bodily feelings that seem to be so important in guiding our actions in all areas of our lives. We realized that our society has a bias against feelings. The only feelings that are formally taught in our society are bladder and rectal pressure. Labels like "coward" and "crybaby" are used for people who acknowledge and express feelings like fear and sadness. This bias seems to be a manifestation of the basic human dilemma – the tension that exists between our society and our biology.

We are born with bodily feelings. We act on these feelings from the earliest moments of life. As we learn to talk, we learn labels to attach to these feelings. As we get older we are taught rules about how we are allowed to act on our feelings and at that point something very important happens which may well determine whether or not we are likely to later develop physical and psychological difficulties. If we are taught that our bodily feelings are normal occurrences and are taught how to act on them in socially acceptable ways, we are unlikely to develop problems related to these feelings. We can come to value our feelings, use them as guides in living, and allow them to enrich our lives. On the other hand, if we are taught that it is socially unacceptable to act on our feelings, we are at risk for developing physical and/or psychological problems. And, if we are taught that even having emotions is unacceptable we are almost certain to develop significant problems.

Heidi Sauder and her colleagues have written an excellent little book that takes what we've learned about body sensations, physiology, and emotions, and makes it available to any woman (men will benefit from reading it too!) who is interested in learning more about her body with the goal of becoming more effective in planning, problem-solving, in relationships, and enriching her life. The reader is given a clear explanation of some of the most important body sensations as well as simple, practical, and effective techniques for learning to be more aware of the feelings, understand what they mean, and use them to act more effectively in their lives. This is a book that I've been waiting for. It will be required reading for patients (and staff!) in our interdisciplinary chronic pain rehabilitation program. Feelings are our biological heritage. Read this feelings owner's manual to learn more about them and experience the joy of being in touch with the fullness of your being!

Ed Harpin, Ph.D.
Sharp Chronic Pain Rehabilitation Program
San Diego, California

INTRODUCTION

Feelings occur for a reason. They serve to help you understand situations and to guide your behavior. Unfortunately, many people don't understand what they feel. This book has been written to help you identify what you are feeling by paying attention to your internal body sensations. Making a habit of paying attention to these sensations will make it possible for you to understand what you are feeling. Once you fully understand what you feel, you will be able to respond in a way that fits the situation and can accurately reflect your goals and desires.

I am a neurologist who began my career as a headache specialist. I was particularly interested in tension headache, and I asked the question, "What is tension?" In the beginning I realized that tension involved our muscles but it was then that I ran into a perplexing problem. It was well-known by neurologists that during a tension headache, a patient's muscles are not in spasm, they appear normal on all tests. I discovered that the muscle abnormality is not in the muscles themselves but in a small structure inside the muscle called the muscle spindle. Although the main job of the spindle is to tell the brain how stretched the muscle is, the spindle also responds to emotion.

When I began treating patients with tension headache I discovered that these patients were unable to tell when they were tense. At the Sharp Pain Rehabilitation Clinic in San Diego and then at MyoPoint Pain Disease Management, my wife Arlene P. Hubbard, M.S., O.T.R., and I discovered that patients with tension headache were not only unable to tell if they were tense, they were also unable to tell when they were annoyed, or irritated or angry. We were able to help them reduce their muscle tension by teaching them to notice the sensation in their bodies when they were tense and how to reduce it.

When we treated patients suffering with migraine, which is entirely different from tension headache, we made a similar discovery. Patients with migraine also were not skillful at noticing a body sensation, only this time it wasn't tension, it was anxiety and fear. They didn't understand what the body's sensation of anxiety felt like unless it was extremely severe!

This was very important, because anxiety constricts blood vessels. That's why migraine patients typically have cold fingers and hands, since the blood is not flowing well into them. This is similar to what happens in the brain before a migraine attack. (The classic symptom of migraine is first a change in vision, called a prodome, then a headache that starts quickly, often within an hour or two, and last several hours or even a day, usually accompanied by nausea. Tension headache on the other hand, is typically more or less continuous, fluctuating during the day.)

In migraine the blood is shunted, or detoured, from the brain into the lining of the brain called the meninges (where the term "meningitis" comes from). Like tension headache patients, migraine patients can reduce the frequency of their attacks by recognizing the sensation of anxiety that precedes the attack.

In this book you will learn how to recognize the body sensations of all feelings. This book will speak about feelings and give ways of identifying them, as well as ideas, for resolving feelings in general terms. Our generalizations are not meant to be diagnostic or serve as a treatment plan for extremely distressing, chronic or habitually damaging patterns of thinking or behaving. If you think you may be experiencing depression, anxiety, or any harmful pattern of thought or behavior, please seek the help of a medical or mental health professional.

David R. Hubbard, MD

WELCOME TO OUR BODYSENSE COMMUNITY

Our goal for you as you read this book is that you will tap into the long forgotten wisdom of your body. A beautiful aspect of your body is that it never lies! It feels what it feels without regard to social rules or the "shoulds" you put on yourself. When you learn how to pay attention and respect what your body is telling you, you will experience the wisdom and relief that comes from knowing your truth and acting on it. The process in this book will take practice but as you take the time to work through the steps it will become second nature. Let's get started!

In this book we will follow four women who began one of our BodySense Workshops together.

Sally, a 55 year-old lawyer, has been married for 27 years to Chris and is the mother of two young children. She tells us she has come to the workshop to find her "spark" and bring some "fun" back into her life.

Sarah just turned 21 and lives at home with her parents while she decides what to do with her life. The college counselor recently recommended that Sarah receive "anger management" counseling after getting into a rather public altercation with a male student at school. She has been dating a guy named Adam.

Rachel is a 35 year-old single woman and military veteran. She says that she is having difficulty starting a new career and wonders if she could be depressed. She has been dating Morgan for a few months.

Brittany is 28 years old, has been married for 3 years to Ed, and proudly declares she is "childfree." She tells us that she is "anxious" much of the time and would like to find out why.

Each of these women comes to our workshop for her own reasons. For the next several sessions they will be learning about their bodies, the feelings within them and most important of all how being aware of their feelings can enrich and improve their quality of life.

GETTING STARTED

Take a moment to check in with your body. Pay special attention to sensations or feelings within your body. What sensations are you able to feel? The sensation of bladder pressure that signals you to excuse yourself to the restroom is one sensation all of us are aware of and pay attention to.

We focus first on the ability to feel bladder pressure, not because it is a glamorous sensation, but because it is a sensation that you are an expert in being able to recognize and respond to. Continue to scan your body for other sensations that you are able to localize, pinpoint and describe.

Scanning your body for sensations, being able to localize sensations and describe them is different than guessing what you are feeling. This book will guide you in scanning the inside of your body for sensations and in using these sensations to know what you feel. Curiosity about sensations within your body gives awareness of feeling; and knowing what you feel is the first step in figuring out what you should do or how you should act in your daily life.

Becoming aware of internal sensations can be illustrated with the example on the following page.

Brittany came to the workshop complaining of 'general anxiety', eating a lot, and gaining weight. As she worked on noticing where in her body she was feeling anxious, she realized that she was specifically feeling a 'racy tumbling' in her gut when thinking about going on a trip with her husband, Ed. This 'racy tumbling' was an uncomfortable feeling for Brittany and she would nibble on food to cover or numb the sensation.

Getting in tune with her body and the sense it gave her pointed to the real issue for Brittany, which was a vague anxiety over a lack of intimacy with her husband Ed. The feeling had nothing to do with hunger. Brittany got curious about her fear of being in situations where she would be "sitting around with nothing to talk about" with her husband. This sensation led her to realize that her marriage had lost some of its connectedness.

Brittany decided to use her body to guide her in planning the upcoming vacation with her husband. When she noticed the 'racy tumbling', she would try different strategies until the feeling resolved. For instance a few days later Brittany arranged for a babysitter so she and her husband could go out for dinner. She told Ed about her realizations. Ed asked her directly if she was still interested in keeping their vacation reservations. Before answering, Brittany checked in with her body and immediately noticed the 'racy-tumbling.' She told Ed the vacation made her uneasy and asked if he would be willing to put the trip on hold until they had had some time to discuss and plan a vacation they would both enjoy together. He agreed and she noticed the sensation subside.

Listening to her body's internal sensations allowed Brittany to figure out what she was feeling which gave her the opportunity to act on her fear of lack of intimacy instead of overeating.

Take a minute to check in with your body.

Describe whatever internal sensations you are aware of:

_____

_____

_____

Illustrate on the figure below where you feel your internal sensations. The descriptors below are just examples to get you started. Feel free to add your own words that match your awareness.

Tightness

Pressure

Lump

Tension

Butterflies

Racey/Queasy

Heaviness

Lightness

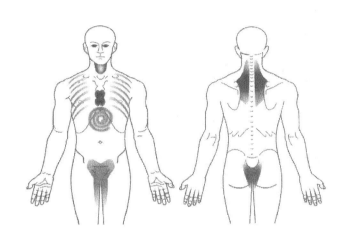

You may be scribbling like mad with a flood of sensation awareness from all over your body. Or, you may be completely numb and have difficulty feeling any sensation at all. Be patient. This book will show you how to become aware of these sensations and know what to do with them.

Begin checking in with your body throughout the day to scan for internal sensations. This takes practice, so be diligent. Check in regularly. You will come to enjoy it!

On the next page is a template you may copy to help you in recording your increasing awareness of your internal sensations. Get in the habit of noticing these sensations. After you have recorded your inner sensations on the following template for a few days, look over your findings. What area or areas of the body have you marked most often? How long does a sensation last? See if you can notice what makes the sensation more intense or what resolves the sensation.

INTERNAL SENSATION AWARENESS RECORDING TEMPLATE

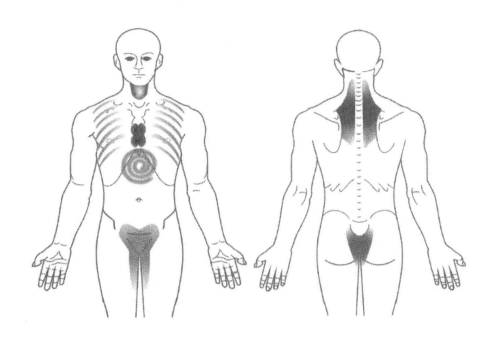

Date: Time of Event: Time of Recording:

Check in with your body.

Mark on the figure where you feel any internal sensation.

What does this sensation feel like? Describe it.

_____

_____

_____

Pay particular attention to when the sensation began. What triggered the sensation?

What makes the sensation more intense?

What makes the sensation less intense?

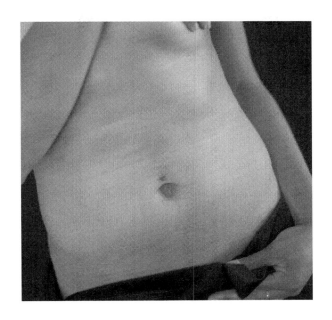

HUNGER

Rachel sticks her head into Cory's office, "Let's do lunch, woman!"
Cory looks up and smiles, "How about 11 o'clock, before the lunch
crowd?" Rachel nods and turns to walk back down the hall, calling
over her shoulder, "I'll stop by then, how about our usual spot?"

Our culture confuses hunger with schedules, food, tastes, textures, and
aromas. We eat when it is lunchtime or when it fits into our schedule or
when someone asks us to eat with them. Perhaps more important, we don't
know when we are not hungry. We eat until our plate is clean or until
others at the table put their forks down.

Are you hungry right now? How do you know? Is it because you are walking down the aisle at the grocery store, looking at a menu, or watching television? Most women can tell when they are very hungry. We get an intense gnawing sensation in our bellies.

When we are just a little hungry there is a hollow sensation in our bellies. And when we have had something to eat the empty sensation goes away. If we eat a little more, we experience "satiety." Most people don't use the term "satiety." We don't really think much about the absence of hunger. We are more likely to continue eating until we "feel full" or maybe keep eating until we're "stuffed."

Paying attention to our body sensations allows us to learn how to eat and feel good, neither starving nor stuffed. If you only eat when you are hungry and stop eating when you are satiated you will maintain your ideal, healthy weight. If you pay attention to the sensations in your belly, you gradually come to prefer the sensation of being just a little bit hungry to the sensation of being just a little bit too full.

Brittany had recently taken on additional responsibilities at work. She found herself moving from one responsibility directly to another during the day. Her drive home was filled with returning phone calls and mentally prioritizing her evening to-do list. Often, Brittany would grab anything in the kitchen she could quickly get her hands on, painfully aware she had not taken time to eat all day. One day she thought to herself, "I go days without eating breakfast and lunch but I keep gaining weight, go figure."

Then one morning, Brittany heard a co-worker talking about a podcast on Body senses and how even simple sensations like hunger are easily felt but often ignored. Brittany instantly realized that the sensation of hunger rarely correlated with her eating. She decided to download the podcast and listen to it on the way into work the next morning.

Brittany began regularly and frequently scanning her belly for the sensation of hunger. She became familiar with the hollow feeling and started letting her body sensations lead her to when and how much to eat. At first it was difficult. Brittany forgot to consult her body before popping candy from a co-worker's candy dish. Or she would be watching television and finish the entire bag of popcorn without checking in to see if she was satisfied before the bag was gone.

Deciding not to be discouraged, Brittany slowly began to look to her body for the feeling of hunger before eating, during eating and following a meal or snack. Over time she realized that she hardly ever "pigged out" anymore and frequently would snack during the day on a few nuts, a stick of cheese, a handful of pretzels or a piece of fruit.

She found that being aware of her body before and during eating made eating more enjoyable. Instead of being almost unaware of what she was putting in her mouth, Brittany began savoring foods and sitting down to eat. She was surprised to find that keeping her body comfortable during the day made her less irritable. Gone were the days of Brittany living in a state of either extreme hunger or being "stuffed."

On the other hand, Sarah actually fears hunger. She wishes she could skip over the section on the body sense of hunger. If she wasn't sitting in the workshop, she admits that she would just "fast-forward" to the next chapter in the book.

We tell her that her desire to avoid even the discussion of the sensation of hunger means she should become more aware of it. Even the thought of paying attention to the sensation of hunger immediately resulted in Sarah's stomach feeling racy. "I'll get fat," she immediately tells herself.

Sarah catches the change in sensation from predominantly the sensation of hunger to the sensation of fear. She decides to get curious about this switch. She begins to scan her body for the hollow sensation in her belly. Interestingly enough, when she feels the sensation of hunger, Sarah finds herself making excuses, "It must be something else. I must be nervous." Then comes the next thought, "I probably am hungry, but I don't want to feel that. I'll get fat." Immediately Sarah is aware that her stomach now feels racy. Sarah realizes that she purposefully ignores the sensation of hunger for fear that if she eats, she will become overweight.

The women in the group are sensitive about Sarah's reported fear of the sensation of hunger and take extra time to encourage her to pay attention to her sensation of hunger and stay focused on that. Although Sarah was hesitant at first, she began paying attention to her sensation of hunger and brainstorming ways of reducing the sensation of hunger without feeling "bloated."

Sarah discovers that when she focuses on how to satisfy the sensation of hunger without thinking that she has to overeat, she is slowly becoming able to notice her sensation of hunger and think through what she could eat or drink to decrease the sensation.

Actions to Take

Our number one action to take for the sensation of hunger is to eat when you are hungry but not eat when you are not hungry.

1. If you pay attention to the sensation of hunger vs. satiety you can easily eat just the right amount. Take small bites and wait a minute or two before the next bite. This is an easy way to know when you've transitioned from hungry to satiated. In fact, by taking small bites you will actually enjoy the tastes and textures of food even more.

2. Pay attention between meals to the sensation of hunger. If, in the middle of the morning, you realize you are hungry, you can either wait until lunch and by then be "starving" and unable to resist wolfing down enough food to feel stuffed, or you can have just a bit of something in mid-morning. The trick is to just have one bite of that power bar or a few nuts and then check again. Scan your belly and ask, "Am I still hungry?" You will be surprised how little food it takes to relieve the feeling of hunger. But remember, if you feel satiated you ate a bit too much and if you feel stuffed you ate way too much!

3. Word of warning: If you find you lack a sense of control over the portions of food you eat, consume large amounts of food in short periods of time and then compensate for eating by throwing up or using laxatives, diuretics or other medications, excessively exercise or fast, you may have an eating disorder. Eating disorders are serious but treatable medical conditions. Please seek help from a medical professional.

4. Be aware of the role hormones play in your eating. Many women report cravings during the week before having their menstruation. Craving food is different than being hungry. Before eating, be diligent and decipher if you are mentally

obsessing on food or if you have the sensation of hunger in your belly.

5. Be mindful if or when you consume alcohol, marijuana or other drugs that alter your awareness of internal body sensations. Without the sensation of hunger it will be easy to consume larger amounts of food.

6. Another word of warning: If you find you are disconnected from your sensation of hunger or anxious when thinking about your belly and eating, have an intense fear of gaining weight, and/or are significantly underweight, you may have an eating disorder. Eating disorders are serious but treatable medical conditions. Please seek help from a medical professional.

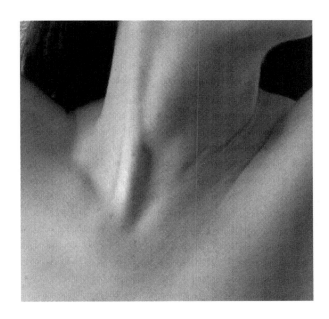

SADNESS

Many women find the feeling of sadness the easiest internal sensation to localize.

> *Sally's four year-old Tasha was sitting beside her mother watching the movie Bambi when she stated, "Mommy, I have a sore throat." Sally looked into Tasha's sweet face and felt her forehead in search of a fever and put her arm around her little girl to comfort her. Tasha buried her face in her mother's chest and burst into tears. The loss of Bambi's mother was too much for her sensitive soul. At four years old, Tasha misinterpreted the lump in her throat as a sore throat, not an internal sensation of sadness.*

Before the tears, there is the lump in the throat that no one else is aware of but you. The lump in your throat is your personal, internal sensation.

The lump can feel extreme, so you can't even swallow, or it can be so mild, so hidden, that you wonder if you must have swallowed too hard.

The lump in the throat is the first clue that you are feeling sad. Knowing you are sad gives you insight on what is going on with you and direction on what actions to take to resolve the feeling. This seems straight forward enough, but many people easily misinterpret what they are feeling.

As Brittany began focusing on her body, she noticed the feeling of a lump in her throat and revealed that she found herself having difficulty swallowing at times. She began tuning into her body and charting situations she was experiencing at the first hint of feeling a lump in her throat. During the workshop, she realized that she was feeling sad at her inability to be 'seen' in her marriage. This awareness allowed Brittany to accurately address a core issue for her which was her sense that she was becoming "too dependent" on her husband Ed. Following the method she was learning in the workshop, she did not focus on the abstract issue of "dependence" but instead stayed with the feeling of sadness. Brittany experimented with how to resolve the feeling of sadness. She remained tuned into her body as she tried new ways of being with her husband. Brittany charted what happened to the lump in her throat when she spoke up or asserted herself instead of remaining quiet or telling her husband what she thought he wanted to hear. Had Brittany continued to misinterpret her feeling of sadness as fear, she would likely have continued to create distance in her marriage instead of building intimacy.

The lump in the throat will tell you unequivocally, absolutely, if you are sad. But, many people get confused about sadness when they focus on what they "should" be feeling.

Most people would agree that one should feel sad at the death of an elderly parent or relative, a friend moving away, or the loss of a beloved pet. All of these situations point to a loss.

However, you may think you should be sad about something that has happened and when you check your body you discover you are not, there is not even a hint of a lump in your throat. Maybe you are somewhat relieved that the friend who is leaving town for a bit is getting out of your hair, or maybe the person who died had been ill and suffering for a long time and you feel relieved, or maybe you are resentful at having cared for an ailing animal for so long.

There was a story in the newspaper last year about a woman whose spouse died in a car crash. She described her experience so touchingly. For a year, she played the role of sad spouse. But then she came out. She had wanted a divorce, she had hated the man, but of course she couldn't admit that, couldn't say so publicly. Until she did, and in the newspaper too!

Sometimes the sense that your body holds is different from how you think you should feel. This happens when our bodies hold truth while our minds function in part on social constraints like what people around us think we should do or feel or how we need to behave. Being aware of this discrepancy is key and allows you to hold the truth that your body informs you of and use your brain to creatively decide what to do about your feelings. This can be enlightening.

Rachel had been using her body to know what she was feeling for months. In fact, she felt like a pro in being able to realize very early on her feelings and address issues successfully. Then one day she told the group that upon scanning her body she noticed a very slight lump in her throat. She immediately thought, "I'm sad." But, then she became confused. Her thoughts swirled, "But there is no reason to be sad, I have nothing to be sad about, my life is great, nothing has happened." Rachel decided to trust the information her body gave her. She got creative and began scanning her experience for subtle clues that triggered her feeling of sadness. Her attention fell on the song playing on the radio and immediately resonated with the lump in her throat. It was a song played often in the barracks during her time in the military. What was it she had lost during this time?

Pay attention to the subtle sadness for it tells us about the day-to-day losses we could best honor more. Subtle sadness can be tearing up when your baby takes her first steps, feeling a sudden lump in your throat as you hear the opening bars to the song you danced to at your wedding, or something as simple as looking in the mirror and seeing wrinkles around your eyes.

Some causes of sadness may seem ambiguous, like the loss of personal identity. We hear many stories from mothers who are now "empty-nesters." This transition can be profoundly sad for women who stayed at home full-time to raise their children. Many tell us they don't know who they are anymore and are sad at the loss of identity. Other common examples of the loss of identity are the loss of a job, a divorce, or leaving a beloved community.

Ambiguous losses can cluster around the sheer passage of time or opportunity. You might have held a dream when you were younger to achieve something special, such as competing in a professional sport, having a baby, or pursuing a particular career path. Now you have come to realize that the time to achieve this dream has expired and you mourn its passing. At times, triggers for these more ambiguous losses can be hard to identify. Be patient and get curious.

When you feel a lump in your throat, you can acknowledge to yourself that you are sad, ask yourself what the sadness is about and scan your environment and current experience for clues. Usually, when the light dawns on the trigger of your sadness, tears well in your eyes. That is a good thing, now you are aware of what you are experiencing and you can deal with it appropriately.

Actions to Take

So what is one to do when they feel sad? Fortunately, the most effective solution for sadness is a natural response. Gazing upon a mournful face or seeing someone crying naturally brings people closer to the person who is sad. Getting close is the natural solution for sadness.

Of course, some causes for sadness may not be resolved in a short period of time. The death of a loved one or the loss of a core personal life dream takes time to resolve. In working through these lengthier resolutions, you may find it helpful to use more than one strategy.

You may also find that you need to limit time for sadness so you can function. Because sadness is about loss, you will notice that many of the activities are related to connecting.

Listed below are suggestions you may add to your brainstorming for ways that you can resolve sadness:

1. Getting close is our number one recommendation to resolve the feeling of sadness. You may choose to connect with a friend or family member who is able to understand you and with whom you are able to share. Talk about what you have lost, how you feel, and what you need. You may also connect with others who have gone through a similar experience. Not only do you make new acquaintances who may become friends but it is also a great way to understand that you are not alone.

2. Keeping a journal may be a resolution strategy for you if you are more comfortable being alone than with friends or family during periods of sadness or if people are not readily available every time you feel sad. Journaling entails writing down your feelings of sadness. Write without censoring yourself. Write in incomplete sentences and don't worry about good spelling or grammar. Get your story on paper. Don't worry if someone else might see it or read it, you can always tear it up, burn it or

destroy your journaling when you are done. Have a box of tissues near by as you write and allow yourself to cry.

3. Sometimes you need to cry. Holding sadness inside causes headaches and stress. So here we go.... Get out the sad music, the tissues, light some candles, and shut the door. Sit down and cry until the tears are gone. Allow yourself to let go and grieve.

4. Volunteering is a way of getting close to the loss we have experienced. A meaningful connection between the loss you experienced and the sadness you feel is a key component of finding resolution of sadness through this strategy. For example, finding purpose at the Humane Society following the death of your beloved pet can be purposeful grieving and help in healing the sadness you feel.

5. Learn the lessons. Pull out your journal and take the time to write down the lessons you have learned from this situation. Write down what you have learned from having gone through this loss, as well as anything you would like to do differently in the future.

6. Find the essence of your dream. If you are sad over the loss of a dream or an identity, take the time to find what you really love and miss about that dream. Perhaps you have been a full-time mom, and your last child left for college. What is it you loved most about being a stay-at-home mom? Was it caring for someone? Was it organizing the household? Sitting at the soccer games and chatting with other parents? Feeling that you mattered to someone? When you look at the important parts of that identity, you will realize that you may still create that essence in your life. You can find a way to use your organizing skills. You can find ways of caring for others, whether volunteering or through a paid position. Make a difference. Whatever dream you have lost, find a way to still have the essence of that dream in your life today.

7. Honor the memories. Nostalgia is a common source of subtle sadness. Remembering a special grandparent, your high school years, or when your children were babies are bitter-sweet moments. Take the time to honor those memories in a way that is meaningful to you. Find a picture and frame it. Start an ancestor wall with pictures of your family, especially those you miss who have passed on. Display items in your home that represent memories you love. Video tape your parents telling stories about their childhood.

8. Turn sadness into positive action. The most touching examples of this are parents who lost children, perhaps to an accident caused by a drunk driver or due to negligence by a company. The parent deals with their sadness by connecting with others and working towards preventing this from happening to another child.

9. Create closeness in your life. Intimate relationships are a natural means to resolve sadness. The exercise on the following page may be helpful in examining closeness with others and increasing intimacy with those you choose.

Examination of Closeness with Others

Make a list of your friends and loved ones. Start with immediate family members and then add relatives, friends, co-workers, and finally people you deal with frequently like a hairdresser.

Enter a number from 1 to 10 in the 'Closeness' column where 1 means "very distant" and 10 means "very close."

Enter a number from 1 to 10 in the 'Preference' column where 1 means "no interest in being closer" and 10 means "very much wanting to be closer."

Now comes the feeling part. Look at each row, one after the other, and while doing so ask yourself what feeling comes to mind? Write your conclusion in the fourth column. If you don't know, write "don't know" or any comment that comes to mind.

NAME	CLOSENESS (1 - 10)	PREFERENCE (1 - 10)	FEELING

Come back to this exercise repeatedly and add to the list often. Having better relationships may be a large part of why you are reading this book. To a certain extent, this book will have helped you if the second and third columns on this list become better matched.

There are three types of intimacy: intellectual, emotional, and physical. Intellectual intimacy is the sharing of beliefs, convictions, and aspirations. Emotional intimacy is the sharing of feelings. Physical intimacy is the sharing of bodies.

If you find it difficult to engage in these steps, or feel completely weighed down by sadness, you may be depressed. Depression is a serious but treatable syndrome and is not a personal failing. Some of the symptoms of depression are a loss of interest or pleasure in activities, feeling fatigued, or having decreased energy, or feelings of guilt, worthlessness, or helplessness. If you have some of these symptoms or think you may be depressed, talk to your doctor, or other qualified health professional to determine if you are depressed and discuss available treatment options.

Practice

Scan the front of your neck for any hint of the feeling of a lump in your throat. Keep scanning periodically throughout the day.

Describe the situation(s) that triggers the sensation of a lump in the throat:

_____

_____

_____

Brainstorm possible solutions. Think about ways you can get close. Be creative.

_____

_____

_____

Choose a solution or combination of solutions and create a plan of ACTION.

_____

_____

_____

Review the outcome. What happened? Where you able to get close? What went well? Would you do anything differently?

_____

_____

_____

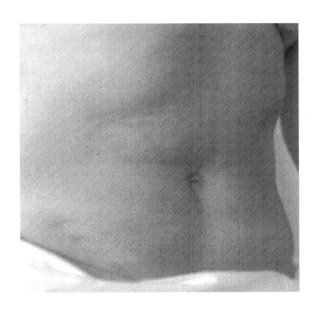

FEAR / ANXIETY

When the group began a discussion of the feeling of anxiety, Brittany told the women that she had been worrying about how long she will have her job. The company had just gone through a round of layoffs and although she wasn't laid off this round, her thoughts circle around being the next to go. She had lost her appetite and in its place was a racy feeling. She realized she was experiencing the feeling of fear.

The racy, queasy gut sensation of fear can be very severe when we are really afraid and it can be so subtle we hardly notice it at times when only a small threat is present. An intense feeling of fear manifests as a feeling of butterflies racing in your gut. When fear is mild it can feel a bit like hunger, or the feeling of too much caffeine. Sometimes fear comes and goes, and other times it remains unresolved and can last for hours. The mild sensation of fear without clear cause is often labeled anxiety.

At the next session, Brittany described an event that week at work. She had noticed her boss' door was closed and immediately felt her heart rate increase and a "racy tumbling feeling in her gut. She checked her pulse as a gym instructor had shown her how to do. She was surprised to discover that her heart rate was normal, even though she was consumed with the intense feeling of butterflies in her stomach.

Brittany's boss emerged from her office and smiled at Brittany. Nevertheless she was still aware of a slight racy feeling and wondered if she should share her worries about keeping her job with her boss. As Brittany got ready for bed that night she wondered what was causing her to feel so anxious. Was she in danger?

Brittany decided she was not in physical danger but felt anxious about the uncertainty of her job, the danger of being out of work. Just knowing that the "butterflies" in her stomach were caused by uncertainty and not some impending danger eased the feeling. Brittany noticed a decrease in the "racy-tumbling" and appreciated not feeling so distressed.

She identified the trigger for feeling anxious and started to brainstorm possible solutions to her uncertain situation at work. At the workshop Brittany learned to keep a small journal by her bed, to write down worries and possible solutions instead of ruminating on them before she went to sleep. She jotted down the option of asking her boss at work how secure her job was. She immediately felt more butterflies racing in her stomach so she continued to brainstorm. Maybe she should allow people at work to see her value by putting herself out there more and publicly taking credit for her work instead of shrinking back from acknowledgement or praise. Brittany was mindful that the "butterflies" were less intense. She decided to act on coming up with ideas and actions for making herself more valuable at work and began to formulate a plan.

What should we do when we are feeling fearful? Sometimes it is tempting to do nothing and just tolerate it. Other times we want to escape it by taking a Valium or having a drink. The best answer when you are feeling fear is to "get safe."

If you are fearful, then you are in danger. The danger may be minor, but your body is reacting to it. Your body is taking it seriously and so should you. Our bodies react to the danger even though we don't consciously interpret the situation as dangerous. This may be because the danger is subtle, an ambiguous threat, like fumbling over your words when you meet someone and believing they will think badly of you. Threat in social situations may be the concern that someone will dislike, disapprove of, or reject you.

Accurately being able to identify the situation that is making you fearful is a key step to knowing what to do to get safe.

Sarah felt on edge. She had been dating Adam for three weeks and frequently felt "butterflies" in her stomach when they were together. At first, Sarah chalked this up to being excited to be with him but the longer they dated, the more she began to wonder what the feeling was about. She decided to pay attention to what was happening when the feeling of "butterflies" first started to come on, monitoring her gut regularly, checking if even a slight unsettled feeling was present.

When Adam picked Sarah up, she kept checking in with her gut throughout the evening. She mentally noted a slight racy feeling when Adam chided her for wearing something "so revealing." He immediately apologized but the sensation only slightly lessened. The sensation intensified when Adam voiced disapproval at Sarah going out to lunch with coworkers, one of which was a male. By the time Sarah got home that night, her head was full of instances of racy-queasy from the evening.

She was tempted to ignore the situations entirely, "How ridiculous!" she thought to herself, "Adam's a generous, and articulate guy, I'm in no danger around him. Maybe I shouldn't be going out to lunch with other people or dressing provocatively." But, what was all the racy-queasy sensation about then? There must be something to this.

Sarah had learned in the workshop that her body didn't lie, there was truth to what she was feeling, and she was curious what truth her body held. She recorded every instance of feeling racy that evening and for the following two dates with Adam. Sarah also made

39

notes of the racy-queasy feeling throughout her day, everyday, for a full week. Saturday morning she sat down with a cup of tea and reviewed all her findings. She noticed the slight racy feeling sprinkled throughout her day when her self-esteem was threatened and more intensely when she was giving presentations at work and feared she would mess up and embarrass herself.

With Adam, Sarah noticed her recordings revealed the intensity of the racy feeling from very slight to uncomfortably intense. She reviewed her notes and could clearly see being with Adam made her anxious when Adam's words or actions were controlling, demeaning, or dismissive. She decided to act on this important body sense. She began brainstorming on her own, and with the group, for solutions to each situation she had recorded.

As taught in the workshop she tried saying to Adam, "I'm feeling a bit anxious right now for some reason." Much to her surprise he looked concerned and attentive and asked her what she was anxious about. Even though she had a pretty good idea, she just said, "I'm going to have to think about it." Adam said "Well I hope it's not because I'm being too pushy." Sarah smiled to herself, thinking that this was a start.

The feeling of fear calls us to accurately identify what triggers the feeling, just as Sarah did in the story above. Generally, the racy-queasy sensation of fear tells us we are in danger and we need to get safe. Other times, we fear what we don't know or cannot control. Examples of this would be your first day on the job or riding a rollercoaster.

"Get safe" depends on accurately targeting the specific situation that triggers your feeling of fear. It is very important to figure out what in particular is causing you to feel fear, and it's not that hard to do. All you have to do is pay attention to the internal sensation, observe when it comes on, and notice what seems to intensify it or lessen it. The closer in time to when the sensation begins the easier it will be for you to figure out what exactly is causing the racy-queasy feeling.

If you are in physical danger, you need to leave the situation, and problem solve on how to keep yourself safe. If stuttering during job interviews triggers your racy-queasy, you would use different strategies to resolve the fear like practicing common interview questions or researching the company. In general, when you are racy-queasy, you need more information before taking action. Use your internal sensation to guide you as you brainstorm possible solutions. Successfully resolving fear will result in the racy-queasy sensation subsiding.

The butterflies sensation that signals fear can be easily felt but hard to resolve. One challenge to resolving the feeling of butterflies is in being able to figure out what triggers it. The dangers in our lives are usually not very dramatic. They are more personal, such as not fitting into your favorite jeans, a higher than usual electric bill, a spouse a bit late from work. Some people may be tempted to say that if the fear triggers aren't dramatic then why do anything about them at all? Resolving even the less dramatic threats in your life is important because your body is reacting to them and because you shouldn't live racy-queasy day in and day out. It's the little dangers that become chronic and debilitating. Why should you have to live like that?

Resolving the racy feeling is also particularly difficult for women who dislike or avoid confrontation. Many women, including the two female authors of this book, fall into the category of conflict avoiders. A situation arises where you fear someone will not appreciate your opinion or become angry at your request and so you keep the thought or idea to yourself. You avoid conflict. Maybe you just label yourself as a 'private' person, or 'introverted' but the racy feeling is palpable.

Women vary in how conflict avoidant they are and with whom they choose to engage in conflict. Some women find it energizing to engage in heated discussions at work but will apologize promptly and profusely with their partners at home for things they are not responsible for.

If you fall into the category of women who avoid conflict, use your body to guide you. At the first hint of anxiety, ask yourself, "What am I afraid of?" Sometimes you may find you are afraid of being embarrassed, or emotionally vulnerable. Other times you might be afraid of being unloved,

41

left, abandoned. Knowing what you are afraid of is an important piece of information so you can plan targeted solutions.

The next step after asking yourself what you are afraid of is to ask yourself, "What do I want?" or, "If I wasn't afraid, what would I ask for?" Two of the most important things to figure out are, "What is the worst thing that could happen and how likely is it to happen?" Thinking about the most catastrophic event may be easy to conjecture, but it is equally important to be able to realistically decide how much of a chance this "great evil" has of actually happening. A great many bad events are possible but only remotely likely to come to fruition.

Sometimes women who are afraid of conflict find it easier to identify and focus on what others in their lives want and need, instead of what they want and need. Letting go of your own needs and wishes is not a solution for the racy sensation of fear. This is a sure fire way of creating distance in your relationships. You may try to convince yourself that you are 'making peace' or 'easing a situation' but in fact, you are avoiding conflict and possibly creating isolation in your relationships instead of closeness.

The solution for the internal racy sensation if you are a conflict avoider is to be able to figure out both what you are afraid of and what you want to have happen. Only then can you choose a solution that matches or balances out your fear and your wish. This can come in the form of stating as quickly as possible to yourself, and possibly the person you are avoiding conflict with, the current problem as you see it and a potential solution.

Sally dreaded the end of the month. Without fail, a racy feeling would build in her tummy as she and Chris would watch their checking account balance dwindle and a stack of unpaid bills gather. Sally had tried to discuss finances with her husband on many occasions, only to feel she had lit a match and thrown it on kindling. The conflict would escalate, with blame tossed about. So she simply avoided talking about money with Chris and tolerated the racy sensation.

The group suggested that Sally shouldn't accept tolerating the feeling of fear and that she might get some ideas by scanning her tummy for the first hint of raciness. When she felt a tinge of racy, she would immediately record the situation. After she had recorded a half-dozen episodes, Sally sat down and read through her notes. Each episode of racy in her tummy had occurred when she felt scared of starting a fight with Chris.

Sometimes the fights were about money but other times she had feared starting an argument about sex or visiting in-laws. Sally sat with the knowledge that she was afraid of making Chris angry. Why was she afraid of Chris becoming angry? She wasn't afraid he would hit her. She didn't feel that she was in any physical danger. All she could come up with was that she was afraid if she made her husband mad he might decide to leave her. This was hard for her to admit, as she felt her marriage to Chris was pretty decent and not at all on the rocks. But in the moment of impending arguing, Sally tended to think only about the worst-case scenario.

Sally took some time to distill what she wanted to happen in each of the situations she had recorded. She wrote down the very things she would have liked to ask for, what she would have liked to say and what she wished for. Her thoughts and wishes didn't seem extreme. Most of the things revolved around feeling loved, having more time, increased understanding of specific wishes, and more openness to her opinions.

Sally noticed that at no point in any of her recorded situations had she given any hint to what she really wanted. In fact, she had never even considered herself in the moment.

She decided to figure out what she wanted and ask for it in the moment in a way that would not likely escalate into a fight. With the group's encouragement, she developed a new strategy: Tell Chris as soon as possible the problem as she saw it and a potential solution that matched her needs.

Conversations around money would go something like this. "Chris, I'm afraid of arguing about money again and want us to work together to figure out a financial plan. Please help me come up with a way we can work on money issues that is productive for us as a couple." Situations around sex began with, "I want to be close to you. Please hug me." Conversations about visiting with her in-laws started with, "I know we have different ideas of how to spend time *with our families. Maybe we can share how we would most appreciate the visit and find some ways of honoring each others' wishes."*

Sally told the group that there was no one-time enlightenment to these differences of perspective. She simply kept telling Chris her viewpoint on what she was feeling or thinking and was open to learning what he might be feeling or thinking in these situations as well. To her surprise, Sally noticed that telling Chris what she was feeling and needing increased the closeness between them. Coming together and increasing closeness came from many discussions of the same topic over time with Sally being willing and able to be open about what she was feeling, instead of "letting it go."

Most women do not live in a fantasy world where everyone around them responds kindly, intuitively, or even unselfishly. Addressing your fear of conflict will likely result in some conflict. Using your body to sense when you are afraid will enable you to decipher exactly what you are afraid of and make it possible for you to tailor solutions to your specific fear.

Actions to Take

So what are you to do when you feel racy-queasy? Getting safe is the natural solution to the feeling of fear. As you problem solve ways of getting safe, feel free to add the following potential solutions to your brainstorming list. Remember, paying attention to when the racy-queasy sensation starts will likely help you brainstorm effective solutions to resolving the feeling of fear.

1. Leave the situation. This may seem too obvious to mention but many people do not think to physically leave the situation that is triggering their racy-queasy sensation.

2. Prepare for the event. If you are racy-queasy before you take a test, you may be afraid of failing. Preparing by studying is one way to resolve the racy-queasy sensation.

3. Get more information to reduce the amount of ambiguity in the situation. Sometimes we fear what we do not know. Getting more information can fill in the gaps in your knowledge and put your body at ease.

4. Do not ruminate on anxious thoughts. Thinking when you feel anxious can make you more anxious as your thoughts can become more catastrophic or worst case scenarios. Write down exactly what is making you feel racy. Problem solve a plan of action and act.

5. Ask for help. Sometimes situations or events are just too big for any one person to handle. We feel afraid of failure and when we listen to our bodies, we are given the chance to ask for help.

6. Find an alternative. Sometimes when you feel racy-queasy it is because you should not be doing what you are doing. Brainstorm other ways of going about getting what it is that you want without making you feel racy-queasy.

7. State out loud what you feel afraid of even if you don't know the solution that reflects your wishes. If you are typically a conflict avoider, this will be a difficult strategy to implement. But it can be as simple as stating "I'm feeling a bit anxious and I'm not sure why."

8. State clearly what you want. Take control of your fear and pursue what would make you feel safe. You may decide to tell someone how to treat you, talk to you, or be with you. You may tell another how to make you feel safe and be a source of comfort instead of a threat.

Try solutions until you are successful.

If you find you are chronically fearful or anxious or are housebound, you may need the assistance of a mental health professional. Speak with your doctor, a psychologist, or other trained mental health professional. Chronic anxiety can be a symptom of an anxiety disorder. Don't be afraid to seek assistance if the steps you are taking on your own do not result in a more manageable life, better relationships, and a healthier mental outlook.

Practice

Scan your body for any hint of racy-queasy sensation in your gut. Keep scanning periodically throughout the day until you are able to feel even a slight racy or queasy sensation.

Describe the situation that triggers the racy-queasy sensation:

_____

_____

_____

Brainstorm possible solutions. Think about what you need to do to get safe. Get creative.

_____

_____

_____

Choose a solution or combination of solutions and create a plan of ACTION.

_____

_____

_____

Review the outcome. What happened? Where you able to get safe? What went well? Would you do anything differently?

_____

_____

_____

HAPPINESS

Sally's chest felt so light she thought it would float away. The hammock hugged her body like a comfortable glove. Every part of her body felt warm except for the hand holding her iced drink. Her gaze rested on the bluest, clearest lagoon far from home and happiness radiated from her chest.

Often we focus on distressing feelings and gloss over or even ignore the pleasant feelings like happiness. Happiness is one of the feelings we need to take extra care to recognize and savor.

Sally shares her memories of her honeymoon in Bora Bora with the other workshop participants. She admits now that thoughts of her once-adored lover are often overshadowed by daily annoyances.

Sally admits to the group that focusing on the feeling of lightness in her chest is not a priority. "When I was dating Chris, happiness was a focal point. I wonder why I changed priorities." The women share episodes of happiness they had experienced over the last week. They muse how easily a light feeling in their chest is shut out by unpleasant sensations.

Sarah chides Sally on no longer looking to her husband for a source of pleasant feeling. The women get quiet for a time, each inquiring within on how they prioritize the feeling of happiness.

As she leaves the workshop session, Sally focuses on the light feeling in her chest and the smile returns to her face. The memory of her husband basking in the sun beside her in Tahiti easily floods her thoughts. Sally recognizes her feeling of happiness and takes the time to enjoy it.

Happiness is experienced by most people as a lightness and expansiveness in the chest. To experience the feeling of happiness you don't even have to be in Tahiti, you can be sitting at your favorite coffee shop, looking upon your firstborn or gazing at the moon and stars. The challenge for many people is that they fail to acknowledge the feeling of happiness at all.

Finding it difficult to feel happiness may be due to the expectation that you're not happy unless you're ecstatic. The feeling of happiness can be subtle, a slight lightness across the chest. More intense feelings of happiness can be experienced as a swelling or expansiveness of the chest. Pay attention to the full range of range of happiness from subtle to intense.

Action to Take

The solution for the feeling of happiness is the simple building of awareness and appreciation for this feeling and taking the time to savor it the feeling within your body. Being mindful of the sweet moments sprinkled throughout most days and feeling happiness allows your spirit to be filled with optimism and hope.

So how do you increase your feeling of happiness?

1. Scan your body throughout the day, being mindful to acknowledge episodes of light expansiveness in your chest.

2. Take the time to enjoy this feeling.

3. Experiment with ways to increase the intensity of the feeling. Dedicate time everyday to spark the feeling of happiness in your body and take the time to savor it. You will be rewarded for this effort because practicing the awareness and appreciation of happiness can help you appreciate all feelings.

4. Tell others when you are feeling happy. Happiness is an ideal feeling to share as a means to increase closeness. Too often we feel happiness for the presence or behavior of another person but fail to tell them so.

Practice

Scan your body for a light, expansive feeling in your chest. Record the situation that triggered this feeling of happiness:

_____

_____

_____

Brainstorm possible ways to savor or increase the feeling of happiness in this situation:

_____

_____

_____

Choose one of the ways to savor or increase the feeling of happiness and create an ACTION plan.

_____

_____

_____

What happened? Notice whether the intensity of the feeling of happiness increased or decreased.

_____

_____

_____

Record two additional situations that likely result in the feeling of happiness for you and be sure to scan your body for the light, expansiveness next time you are in those situations.

_____

_____

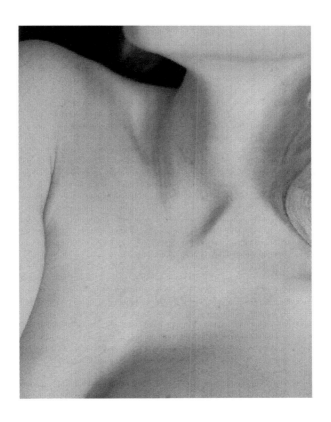

LOVING

Paying attention to body senses now becomes a bit more subtle. In the last chapter we discussed the body sense of happiness, a light, open feeling in the chest. It is difficult to imagine this body sense as anything but positive, and it doesn't require much action. Who wants to "solve" the sensation of happiness?

There is another body sense in the chest that is also open and expansive. One feels it across the open chest, similar to the happiness body sense. We experience this when we are feeling loving toward someone or something. Like happiness, the sensation of loving is a pleasant sensation.

Brittany offers the group an example of her body sense of loving. She and Ed bought a puppy several months ago that they named Boxer. Brittany spent many nights awake with the pup, spent time house training and teaching the puppy not to chew on everything. Sometimes Boxer can be annoying (more on anger/annoyance ahead!). However, Brittany announces to the group, when she comes in the door from work and Boxer runs to meet her, her chest is expansive and light. She says she feels "completely taken in" and cuddles and plays with Boxer, enjoying the sensation in the moment.

Rachel jokes with the group that she wishes feeling loving was as easy when dating. The group shares in her sarcasm and laughs. "Loving in interpersonal relationships can be a bit more complicated!" one of them notes.

The challenge we have with the body sense of loving is not to confuse it with the actions of loving. Other terms for the behavior of loving are doing for others, being selfless, and nurturing. The problem is, being able to tell the difference between feeling loving and acting loving.

When one feels loving there is a natural impulse to act loving. Unfortunately, society and our friends and family expect us to act loving even when we are not feeling loving. Doing for others is usually a good thing, and as a default plan, it is a good idea to be sensitive to the needs of others.

The problem arises when you are doing your best to act loving when you do not feel loving. In fact you may be feeling angry or fearful. This is why you must trust your body. If you are in a situation that seems to call for "acting loving" such as visiting grandparents, or helping out at the local clothing drive, when you are not feeling loving there are a couple of problems you might encounter. The first problem is that others might sense you are pretending to be "nice" and see you as a phony. Another problem with pretending to be loving is that you will be ignoring the feeling you are actually having. Of coarse it is still possible to be helpful even when you are not feeling loving. You might say, "What are you needing that I might be able to help with?" Focus on the specific need of the other person. You don't have to feel loving to help someone!

Sometimes the best thing to do is not to force yourself to act loving but instead be honest about what is going on with you. Say something like, "Let's figure out what is going on with us right now." This allows for you to more clearly understand the other person and for them to understand you. This type of conversation gets to the heart of each other's needs, builds intimacy and often the feeling of love.

Rachel cut in. "Let me tell you, I did that this morning." She went on. "I got a call from Morgan. I noticed that I was slightly racy but I put on the act of being loving. I knew I was feeling irritable, but I thought the right thing to do was act "nice" anyway. The longer I was on the phone and the more loving and generous I was acting, the more racy I got. Finally, I just said that I was running late and had to go. I was totally abrupt, almost rude at the end. Now I don't know what will happen. Just telling the story makes me feel racy again. I was just trying not to hurt her feelings."

"I can tell when people at work are just being 'nice'," Brittany added. "I call it the 'Cheetah Grin', a totally fake smile. It bugs me. Why can't people just shake their head or acknowledge I said something that they didn't agree with?"

Sally was not on board with the discussion. "If I waited for the feeling of loving before I was loving, my family wouldn't know what hit them." All eyes in the group turned to her and she went on, "I'm responsible for keeping people happy. I act loving and caring and nurturing even when I feel tired or irritable. That's what a mother and a wife does."

Silence followed until one of the presenters who was understanding of Sally's position interjected. "Let's take a specific example of what you are talking about Sally, and discuss it as a group. When was the last time you remember acting loving when you were feeling tired or irritable?" the presenter asked.

A huge sigh from Sally was followed by, "This morning as I was leaving for this workshop my youngest daughter wrapped her arms around me and began whining that she didn't want me to go. She went on and on about wanting me to stay at home and cuddle her. I wanted to be loving, comfort her, and get her to let go of me so I could leave. I wanted to act loving but I was feeling frustrated."

The group seemed unanimous that Sally was doing the right thing, but also that she had to validate her frustration as well. Although mothers don't like to think of mothering this way, the fact is that her daughter was manipulating her. Brittany suggests, "How about getting the babysitter to help distract your daughter while you leave quickly or setting expectations with the child ahead of time? Rachel interjects, "How about sitting out of reach on the kitchen counter until your daughter stops bugging you?"

Loving is a pleasant sensation to feel but can be a tricky sensation to honor. You must rethink your tendency to act in a loving way because you think you "should" or because you think other people expect you to. Ideally, how you act will match what you feel.

When your actions reflect how you feel, you are being honest. You are not leading another person to believe you feel something you do not. Acting loving when you feel loving will give your friends, family, and lovers the ability to trust you and know you. Acting loving only when you feel loving makes you a genuine person in your close relationships.

Actions to Take

1. Be aware of when you feel loving. Take the time to notice whom or what you are loving. Savor these moments. In particular, when you are feeling loving, make sure you tell yourself and if possible the person you are loving your feeling. Don't worry that the other person will get tired of hearing it, they can tell you, "enough is enough." If you feel loving, consider telling the person, "I am loving you right now." This is different than "I love you," which can mean that you love the person but may not be feeling loving in the moment.

2. Foster the feeling of loving in your life. Keep track of when you are feeling loving and do things to grow these experiences. Look for the feeling of loving when you are with someone that you care about. Increase how frequently you make contact with those you love.

3. Create opportunities to feel loving. Often we allow our lives with our friends, family, partners, and children to crowd out the feeling of loving. Hectic schedules and multiple roles can create feelings of frustration. Go out of your way to create situations that allow you to feel loving.

4. Be aware when you are tempted to act loving but are not feeling loving. You must acknowledge to yourself that you think you "should" act loving but you are not feeling loving. In these situations where it is expected that you act loving but are not feeling loving, it may be appropriate to be courteous, polite, or quiet, rather than mislead another person or appear "phony."

Practice

Scan your chest for any hint of the feeling of openness and lightness. Keep scanning periodically throughout the day.

Describe the situation(s) that triggers the sensation of openness and lightness in your chest:

_____

_____

_____

Brainstorm possible actions you can take to savor this feeling or create situations that will trigger this feeling. Be creative.

_____

_____

_____

Choose a solution or combination of solutions and create a plan of ACTION.

_____

_____

_____

Review the outcome. What happened? Where you able to feel loving? What went well? Would you do anything differently?

_____

_____

_____

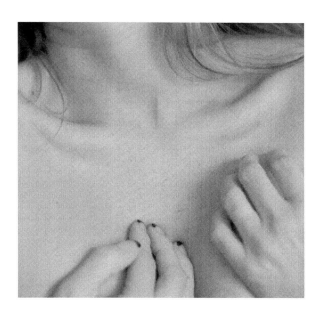

HEARTACHE / LONGING / WANTING

Rachel had been dating Morgan for six months. She lived for the next moment she could stare into her lover's eyes. But then her lover left for business in Europe and wouldn't be back for almost a month. For days and days she plodded aimlessly through her work and chores, with a heaviness settled in her heart.

Heartache is an uncomfortable internal sensation that is brought about by wanting something you cannot have. You long after it, you want it, but it is not to be had. We use the word 'heartache' throughout this chapter but you can substitute 'longing' or 'wanting' as these are different words women use to describe the same internal sensation.

You can feel heartache from many situations. We associate heartache with being in love with someone you cannot have. The reasons you can't have them may vary. The person may not be in love with you, or they may be married to someone else or live far away. Other examples of heartache are missing an old friendship that dissolved, heartache for a deceased loved one or wanting the companionship of your recently deceased pet.

Heartache feels like heaviness in your chest. It may feel as though someone is pressing his or her fist into the middle of your chest. When it is severe, it can be crushing and you may find it difficult to breath. You might even wonder if you are having a heart attack. Like all the other feelings, it fluctuates in intensity, sometimes it is so severe you can think of little else, other times it lingers in the background of your awareness.

Many people think of sadness and heartache as the same feeling, but they are not.

When Sally was pregnant with her first baby, every night she had a dream about her dad who had died in an accident five years earlier. These dreams typically involved Sally's dad helping her with some sort of problem or another. Upon awakening each morning from one of these dreams, she would feel heaviness in her chest. One morning she lay in bed thinking through the dream from the night before, the helpfulness of her father to her and the easy smile on his face in the dream. The heaviness became weightier. Sally's thoughts then changed to how she would never see her father again and how he would not meet her soon-to-be-born daughter. A lump in her throat formed, and tears filled her eyes. This was the moment Sally learned longing and sadness were separate feelings. She felt a fist in the chest and heartache for her father when thinking about the role he played in her life and felt sadness and a lump in her throat when considering the loss of him forever.

Heartache and sadness often come together but don't let this confuse you. Heartache and sadness are distinct and separate feelings. Sadness is the lump in your throat whereas heartache is the heaviness in your chest. Localizing where in your body you are feeling and being mindful of what you are feeling makes it possible to identify heartache from other sensations.

Another sensation that needs to be distinguished from heartache is love. Heartache and love are often two sides of the same coin. After all, we feel the heavy, fist sensation in our chest that is heartache and we feel the open, expansiveness of love in our chest as well. These are separate feelings.

Sarah shared with the group an example from her life when she felt extreme longing. She had been dating Greg for two years and to be honest the last year of their relationship was pretty rocky. Greg finally broke up with Sarah and quickly began dating someone new. When they first broke up Sarah felt relief and then found she longed for him. The longing was especially intense in the evening and on weekends. Sarah thought she was feeling this way because she still loved Greg. Now as she looks back she realizes that she was feeling longing, not loving for Greg. She was longing for companionship and the fun weekends they used to have together.

The sensation of heartache is an uncomfortable feeling. Like all feelings, when heartache is severe there is a tendency to want to do something drastic. You might have found yourself doing stupid things. For the rest of this section, let's use the example of being in love with someone who is not in love with you, or, "just not that into you," as the book and movie put it.

A common reaction is to make a fool of yourself, calling and emailing constantly, scheming to just happen to run into him. If you are unmindful of the feeling of longing and how your behaviors either intensify this feeling or decrease its intensity, you may get into trouble or embarrass yourself. This can range from talking endlessly about him to your girlfriends, to leaving him 20 text messages to stalking him.

If you pay attention to your body you will find that these behaviors intensify the feeling of heartache, not resolve it. Another strategy that might seem attractive when feeling heartache is to run from it. You may throw yourself into a new, but doomed, relationship. Ever had a rebound?

In our example of heartache for someone you cannot have, you find yourself in a state of wanting, dissatisfaction. It is somewhat like sadness but different. When you are sad, you need to "get close." As we discussed in the sadness chapter, when you are crying, other people, even strangers, are drawn to you and will come over to ask you what's wrong.

Sadness has the function of bringing caring people to you. It may be tempting to try to use the same strategy for longing, but longing is different from sadness. You can't bring the person to you no matter how much you'd like to. If you try it you will discover that it doesn't work to try to bring a substitute close. Not another person, not even a close friend. It actually aggravates the chest-in-your-fist sensation.

Actions to Take

Ok, so how does one resolve heartache? We are not going to tell you "it just takes time," or "you just have to learn to accept it." Our strategy is different and effective. Be less self-centered and think about and do more for others.

Strangely, when you are in this state of wanting, you are entirely self-centered, almost narcissistic. The most effective resolution for heartache is to love what you long after. This is hard to understand at face value. You reflectively tell yourself that you love the person or thing you long after, that is why you experience heartache. We are talking about unselfish loving of what you long after.

Focus on how you love or what you love about the person you long after. Focusing on loving the person and what is best for them is likely to resolve the heartache because it is outward focused instead of self-centered.

The following are some examples of solutions to resolve heartache to get you started.

1. Our number one strategy to resolve heartache is to love what you long after. This may seem convoluted or counterintuitive. But it works. Focusing on loving resolves wanting because wanting is different than loving. If someone chooses not to be with you, if you focus on loving them you will naturally focus on what they want and not your own wanting. Force yourself to contemplate and honor their wishes, values, and decisions. Focus on what they want instead of what you want. Remember they must have good qualities or you would not want them in the first place.

2. Do something for someone else. You need to go out and volunteer your time for someone or something greater than yourself. Go to the nearest dog shelter and help out for a few hours. You don't have to promise to make it a lifelong project, you just have to do it.

3. Grow meaningful relationships with family and friends. This is not the same thing as distracting yourself with transitory flings, this is about growing relationships of worth. You may find that you have put little time or effort into knowing what is important to the people closest to you. Did you even remember to acknowledge their birthday or a major life accomplishment they achieved? Get curious about what hurdles they are facing and what kind of meaningful support you could lend. Do something active to acknowledge goals or values they have set for themselves. If you are unsure of what these values and goals are, find out.

4. Develop work. You can increase your productivity at your job. Maybe you need a certification or credentialing to further your career. Actively pursue that critical development. If the majority of your work is taking care of your home, you can organize a closet that has gotten out of control or redecorate an area of your home to reflect your current tastes. Maybe you would like to learn to cook a particular ethnic food or better pair wine with food. Take a class in an area that would further develop your work.

You can use the energy of your aching heart to be productive and outgoing. As you actively pursue loving, volunteering, growing relationships of worth, or developing work, monitor the chest-fist. Be mindful of what intensifies the sensation of heartache and what resolves it.

Practice

Scan your chest for any hint of the feeling of weight or heaviness.

Describe the situation that triggers the sensation of weight or heaviness in the middle of your chest:

_____

_____

_____

Brainstorm possible solutions. Think about how you may be self-absorbed and need to get out of yourself for a time. Consider ways or an area you may be able to love, volunteer your time, build relationships with family and friends or be productive at work. Get creative.

_____

_____

_____

Choose a solution or combination of solutions and develop an ACTION plan.

_____

_____

_____

Review the outcome. What did you do? What happened? What went well? Would you do anything differently?

_____

_____

_____

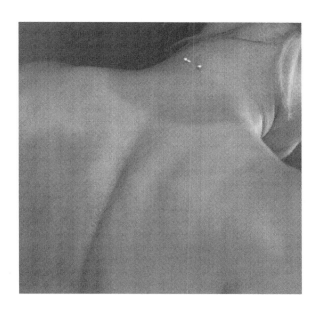

ANGER / IRRITABILITY

Let's talk about anger. If 'anger' is an intimidating word for you, consider the less intense feelings of anger like irritability and annoyance.

Think back to when you were a kid. When was the first time you remember feeling angry? How did your parents respond to you? Could your parents tell when you were angry? How did you know your mother or father were angry?

How you were raised is likely to have an effect on how you think about anger. Some people were raised to think about anger in moral terms of good or bad, right or wrong. Some people were taught to hide their anger, while other people were raised to express it. People also vary in how comfortable or uncomfortable they are with feeling anger.

Anger is one of the feelings with the most moral baggage. Many women just don't feel safe being angry. They were raised thinking, "It's just not right to be angry," or "Nice girls don't get angry." These individuals grew to think about anger as bad. So instead of admitting they are angry, they tell themselves that they are sad, anxious, numb, or depressed.

Being able to name that you are angry is the first hurdle in working with this feeling. You can practice getting comfortable with the feeling of anger by embracing the function anger plays in human interaction. Anger serves to let us know when we need to take care of ourselves by alerting our body to a trespass against us. Being aware, through the feeling of anger, of when someone has 'crossed the line' allows us to take care of ourselves and work towards getting the best out of people we relate with.

Once you are able to simply acknowledge that you are angry, your next step is the opportunity to resolve this feeling. If you were raised in a family of "yellers" maybe you are afraid to express anger for fear of losing control or making a scene. On the other hand, if you were taught to "suffer quietly" you may hide your anger from others and even find it difficult to admit to yourself when you are angry.

Often people find that when they feel angry they are either extremely passive or too aggressive. Both of these ways of behaving are labeled by people as "bad" and so they view feeling anger as "bad" too. The interesting point with this line of thinking is that neither of these approaches addresses your ability to manage, express, or resolve the feeling of anger.

If you had to choose between feeling happiness or anger for 30 minutes, which would you choose? Why? Most people experience feeling anger as uncomfortable. Because no one likes feeling uncomfortable, many people try to deny feeling anger. The problem with this strategy is that choosing not to resolve the feeling of anger allows this feeling to nestle in and permeate.

Brittany sat down with her holiday planner. She could barely recall how it happened but for the past few years her home was center stage for entertaining family for the holidays. She sighed as she began making shopping lists and mentally began calculating the financial responsibility.

A few years ago it was just Brittany, her sister and their parents to plan for; this time was full of rich creativity for her. Brittany rubbed the back of her neck and began to wonder if she was just "burned out." She did not want to spend another holiday season with a nearly ever-present headache.

Instead of menu planning, Brittany sat down and tried to pinpoint what made her feel tense between her shoulder blades. She jotted down the financial cost, the time spent preparing, and the energy to accomplish the added entertaining in addition to her already full schedule. She found herself wondering why she was doing all the work and bearing the whole financial load.

Didn't anyone think of helping out? Why should she have to scrimp and save and no one else contribute? This was it! She was able to easily see how the initial joy of entertaining had given way over the years to feeling impinged upon and taken for granted.

But what was she to do? She had volunteered for the responsibility years ago and couldn't see herself confronting her family. Brittany figured she would just have to push forward and press through the holiday. She took a glass from the cupboard and some aspirin to lessen her headache.

Since it is tempting for many people to not want to identify that they are angry, how do we know when we are angry? We know by observing our bodies and by noticing where in our bodies we are experiencing our feelings. So where do you feel it in your body when you are feeling angry? Next time you think you are angry or annoyed or tense observe your body and sense where you feel it.

Many people discover a tightness between the shoulder blades. At first it might be barely noticeable, a slight pulling sensation. As it builds it can become a burning sensation and eventually it actually becomes painful. If you have neck pain, from an old whiplash injury for example, you will discover that the tension between the shoulder blades will spread into the areas of neck pain and make it worse.

If you suffer from muscle tension headache, you will discover that these headaches are also aggravated by the tension between the shoulder blades if it persists for more than an hour or two. Paying attention to the area between your shoulder blades can clue you in to when you are angry, because you will be able to feel it.

Common situations that make us angry and create tension between our shoulder blades are when someone trespasses against us.

Here is what Sarah said:

I was meeting a friend for dinner and was standing by the maître d' station 10 minutes past the reservation time with no friend in sight. Checking my watch for the third time, I'm glancing around restlessly. That's when I felt a tightness between my shoulder blades.

Finally my friend breezes in all smiles and full of excuses. Plastering on a smile, I tell my friend that it is no big deal. The tightness between my shoulder blades intensifies. I find myself being short with my answers and abrupt in replies. My friend asked if everything was all right, saying, "You don't seem like yourself tonight."

Sarah said she assured her friend that she was fine, that she just had a busy week. Very soon she began to wonder why she was feeling irritable. She tried to identify the source of her tension. She realized it had begun when she was standing in the lobby waiting, waiting, and waiting for her friend to arrive. The tense feeling between her shoulder blades told her that she was experiencing anger.

This example may seem small. You may tell yourself, that it 'doesn't matter' or 'it's not a big deal'. We disagree. Our philosophy is that all internal sensation is information for you to be able to understand and then use to decide how you want to handle a situation.

Telling yourself "it's not a big deal" doesn't make you less irritable. Your body tells you that you have been trespassed against and you are called to act. The key to managing anger in a way that is consistent with your values and ideals is to catch the feeling of anger early on, before it gets more uncomfortable and difficult to resolve.

Sally tells the group about making dinner the other night with her husband Chris. Chris starts picking at the vegetables that are being prepared. A small tension creeps between her shoulder blades. She doesn't say anything but finds herself using more force then necessary as she closes cupboard doors and sets pots down!

She tells herself, "He's had a hard day and I should just let it go." The tension grows. Sally is aware of the increasing intensity of the tension between her shoulder blades and knows this is her body's signal to "get equal", an expression she learned in the workshop. She considers possible options and decides to act.

She really doesn't feel like giving him the silent treatment all night. "You know I get annoyed when you pick at the food before I'm finished preparing it." That's all she says and her tension melts a bit. Unfortunately, Chris chooses to become defensive, and says, "Don't be so touchy." The tension creeps back in between Sally's shoulder blades because she once again feels trespassed against.

Sally thinks on how to be straightforward and resolve the issue. Nothing comes to mind and she calmly leaves the room to decide how to deal with her husband. Once she's had some space to think, she enters the kitchen and simply tells Chris that she doesn't want to fight or have their dinner ruined, she simply needs to be treated as an equal and have her space in the kitchen respected. He nods and is silent for a few minutes but then walks up behind her at the sink and offers to take out the trash for her. "It's a good start," she thinks to herself.

Learning how to deal with these small situations to resolve anger, and practicing your action skills is a powerful way of keeping relationships on track and encouraging other people to treat you respectfully. People will acknowledge you as self confident and assertive and you can feel strong in honoring yourself and your wishes.

Another major benefit from not allowing other people to trespass against you is that you keep destructive patterns from developing. Clients tell us all the time they wish they had listened to the clues that their abusive partner was controlling, or how they wished that they had "said something earlier" before a situation escalated.

Your body signals very early on that one of your boundaries has been breached and if you listen and respond, you can spare yourself destructive relationships. Set limits or boundaries with people. Parents intrinsically know this. The sooner and more firmly they set limits, the better their children behave.

Honoring ourselves and dealing with the little trespasses early on with people in our lives keeps situations small, manageable and builds respectful relationships.

> *Brittany tells the group about a co-worker who consistently dumps his workload on others. Brittany said she got tired of feeling the tension between her shoulder blades that resulted from her getting "suckered into" doing his work and decided to act. She told her co-worker that she would "trade" responsibilities in turn for completing his reports. The requests from this male co-worker dwindled. However, Brittany reported that another co-worker in the office had been "targeted" to pick up the report completion. Brittany overheard the co-worker badmouthing the "lazy guy" over the water cooler. Instead of setting boundaries with the "lazy" co-worker, the other woman decided to complain but was still "stuck" with his work.*

It is easy to explain away and not pay attention to small trespasses. We are tempted to mistrust our bodies. For instance, people often say, "Why should I be angry? There's nothing to be angry about!" Again, with practice you will find your body doesn't lie and you are called upon to set boundaries even in small ways.

Sarah was the first workshop member to talk about her headaches. She had had chronic daily headaches for several years prior to coming to the workshop. She had been told they were migraines although she never saw "auras" nor experienced nausea with the headache. As she began monitoring tension between her shoulder blades she discovered that unresolved tension between her shoulder blades resulted in a headache at the back of her head, moving around to her jaws and forehead over the next several hours.

She started becoming aware when the tension began and noticing what was going on around her. She told us that her desk at work was in close proximity to the copy machine and that when coworkers came to make copies they would utilize her desk as a catchall. That is when the tension would begin.

Sarah was hesitant to do anything about this situation. She told herself "it wasn't a big enough thing to make a stink about." Her headaches continued. The group helped her problem-solve solutions and she finally came up with a creative one that was assertive but not confronting. She re-arranged her desk so that others were unable to place their paperwork on her desk.

She discovered that this daily source of tension was completely eliminated. Although it was not her only source of tension, this strategy removed one of the significant causes of worsening headaches in the afternoon at work.

Creative or simple actions are often able to resolve anger without much fuss.

Sally also got neck and low back pain, although not on a daily basis. She had postponed sitting down to plan the family holiday until one day when her sister called to check in on the details. She was tempted to make an excuse for not having the times available. With the group's encouragement, Sally finally decided to discuss with her sister the awareness that planning the family holiday was no longer filled with joy and creativity and that instead she felt burdened and taken for granted.

There was silence on the other end of the phone and Sally worried she had made the situation worse. Then her sister offered this, "Sis, I just never wanted to offend you. You are the creative one in the family and since you volunteered, I never wanted to step on your toes by taking on some of the responsibility. I can imagine how much work you go through and can assure you I appreciate it. I am also happy to contribute my share and will make calls or send emails to the rest of the family so they are able to help out as well."

Sally was the silent one now. Her first impulse was to apologize and tell her sister that everything was fine and that she would do it alone again but Sally listened to her body and refused to spend another holiday season with a persistent headache. So she thanked her sister and told her that she very much appreciated her willingness to help out and the reassurance that her work did not go unnoticed.

Sally discussed with her sister different ways of the family helping out and both she and her sister made phone calls enlisting assistance from the family to make for a truly joyous event. Sally even decided to ask the children of the family to help out, by making the table decorations. For the oldest member of the family, Sally requested they bring the family together through a story recounted between dinner and dessert. Sally had her first holiday without being in pain and it appeared that everyone had more fun with this simple but effective change.

Actions to Take

If you are not used to asking for what you need or setting boundaries, and instead tend to be rather passive in life, finding a personal style to resolve the feeling of anger may take you some time to develop. You may find that you become extreme in your responses at first. If your normal response is to do nothing, you may find yourself exploding.

Sometimes the only options to a problem seem to be one extreme or the other. Often, the extremes are not your best or only options. Get curious and brainstorm creative solutions. Look for possibilities that are not extreme and that are truthful and in keeping with your values. Be kind to yourself at this stage. This ability to ask for what you need and set boundaries requires practice, and you may find it helpful to review the results of your various solutions for effectiveness and fine-tune your style over time.

1. Set limits or boundaries. This is our number one solution for resolving the feeling of anger. Consider telling the other person what you need or what boundary you want them to respect.

2. Act early on, while the feeling is small. Being aware of when the tension between your shoulder blades begins will allow you to act early on and reduces the likelihood that you will have to resort to something extreme, like yelling or saying something curtly. Acting early on will also keep you from minimizing small trespasses that add up and make it impossible to figure out what triggers your latest blow up at someone you love.

3. Ask for what you need. Sometimes we experience tension between our shoulder blades, not because someone intended to make us mad but because they simply didn't know what we wanted. Asking for what you need will clue others into your needs and wishes and not force them to simply guess or rely on their own value system in relating to you.

4. Sometimes the "solution" is just stating the sensation you are aware of. "I feel tense when I hear you say that" can be effective at resolving tension.

Practice

Scan your body for any hint of tension between your shoulder blades. Keep scanning periodically throughout the day until you are able to feel a slight pulling or sensation of tension.

Describe the situation that triggers the sensation of tension:

_____

_____

_____

Brainstorm possible solutions. Think about what boundary you need to set or what you need to ask for. Remember to consider less extreme solutions. Get creative.

_____

_____

_____

Choose a solution or combination of solutions and create an ACTION plan.

_____

_____

_____

Review the outcome. What happened? Were you able to set a boundary or ask for what you needed? What went well? Would you do anything differently?

_____

_____

_____

If your anger results in rage or if you find that you are chronically irritable, you may need the assistance of a mental health individual. Speak to your doctor, a psychologist, or other trained mental health professional if the safety of yourself or people around you is at risk when you are angry. Chronic irritability can also be a symptom of depression and anxiety. Don't be afraid to seek assistance from a mental health professional if the steps you are taking on your own do not result in a more manageable life, better relationships, and a healthier mental outlook.

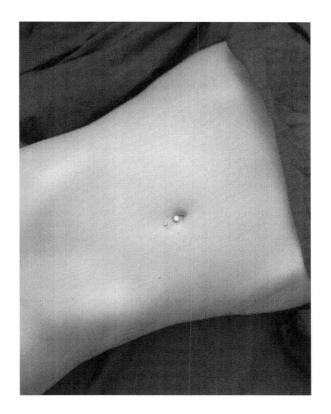

SEXUAL AROUSAL

What does sexual arousal feel like? Are you sexually aroused right now? How do you know? If you are sitting and reading this book now you are not likely to be sexually aroused.

Do you remember the last time you were sexually aroused? This is a trick question, because we are not asking about the last time you had sex. Different question isn't it? As with most everything in this book and our workshops and podcasts, we make the distinction between what you feel and what you do. The hope is that you are learning how to better match what you do with how you feel.

You can remember the last time you had sex because sex tends to be not entirely an everyday routine and to have memorable components. But can you remember the last time you were sexually aroused? One might assume that these would go together, but if you stop for a moment you realize that they may not, at least maybe not perfectly.

Talking about what sexual arousal feels like proved an uncomfortable topic to discuss for the workshop group. There was silence followed by all the ladies looking at the floor when asked to describe the body sense of sexual arousal. We helped them out and described the body sense of sexual arousal as a warm and tingling sensation in the groin, which spreads to the belly and inner thighs.

> *Rachel tells the group the first time she realized the difference between arousal and different kinds of sexual activity was after dinner at her home when Morgan playfully offered to wash her hair. Morgan sat on the edge of the bathtub while Rachel settled in to the warm water and closed her eyes. She felt her fingers just lightly touch her scalp and it changed everything. She felt her tenderness, her patience, and her interest in making her feel good. The relationship really took off that night, emotionally and physically. It was incredibly arousing but different from her usual expectation of what sex was supposed to be like. For one thing, she enjoyed Morgan lightly tracing her wet body, beginning on her neck and slowly down between her legs without ever touching her labia and without the pressure to just "get off." "Orgasms are fine, but what I really want is intimacy, yes physical but especially emotional intimacy," she asserts. Another stunned silence from the group. "Me too," says Sally. "I agree," says Brittany.*

Like all body senses it can be almost unnoticeable or it can be so strong it is almost painful. A sudden feeling of blood rushing into the labia, feeling the vagina wet and small fingers like electricity bolting through the lower belly are all body senses of sexual arousal. If it has been some time since you have had the sensation of tingling in your belly, recall the feeling in your belly during a sudden dip in the road while traveling or being on a rollercoaster during the downward rush, or swinging on a swing at the park. Women may discover they feel some of the sensations of arousal, like wetness, often while they don't feel other sensations, like fingers of warmth in their belly, very often at all. In fact, many women may not feel any of the sensations of sexual arousal until they are already having sex or they may feel all of the sensations of sexual arousal while not even thinking about having sex.

> *Sarah told the group that she had sex at her boyfriend's request, not because she herself was aroused. In fact, she admitted that there were times she wasn't aware of being aroused at all even while they were having sex.*
>
> *Brittany, on the other hand, said that she was very aroused when she was having sex but had discovered she didn't start getting aroused until she was actually in the act. Her husband seemed to be easily aroused, but she found she needed to "get into it."*
>
> *The group discussion turned from what sexual arousal felt like to how you could make yourself sexually aroused. What would stimulate sexual arousal? Rachel joked that for men that was easy, there is a whole industry, called pornography.*
>
> *The group agreed that it was easy for a man to tell if he was aroused because of his erection. It is all outside of the body and hard to hide. Talking about the penis proved easy for the group of women.*

The penis is not a muscle, and it is not under voluntary control. There is a muscle attached to the belly wall so that a man can voluntarily make it twitch up a bit, but that's it. An erection is caused by engorgement or an involuntary increase in blood into the penis and that's what makes it stiff.

For women it is not so simple. The physiological changes are subtler. But women also have engorgement of their vagina, labia, and clitoris, with swelling, warmth and fluid secretion, or lubrication. Woman's engorgement and lubrication is much less visible, less obvious.

In addition, women are easily able to keep their sexual arousal private, a secret, even from themselves.

Rachel speculates that many women are just too modest or perhaps think it's socially taboo to look for their own sexual arousal and for some women it may be socially taboo to be aroused.

It is important to honor each of your feelings whether you are comfortable with them or not. This includes the feeling of sexual arousal. Each of our feelings, when honored will give important information that will wisely guide our actions. The first step to honoring feelings is being able to identify them and then making decisions on what we to do with them or about them.

Lack of Arousal

Sally told the group she missed being sexually aroused. She missed the excitement, vitality and how her body felt. Her husband, Chris, is happy with their marriage, likes that she teases him and that she satisfies him as often as he wants without complaint.

Does he wish she was sexually aroused? She tells the group about a fairly regular occurrence around her home. She describes watching Chris step out of the shower. He quickly dries off and ties the towel around his waist. Noticing that Sally is awake, Chris walks over to their bed and kisses Sally good morning.

Playfully teasing, Sally takes the towel and opens it slightly to expose Chris. He laughs and jokes, "Careful there." Sally immediately notices her husband becoming firm and teases back, "Hey, what's this? I'm just looking at it." He laughs and walks back into the bathroom to get ready for work, turning around while rounding the corner to flash her.

Sally calls back to him, "I'm looking at it," aware that he is now fully erect. "I'm looking at it" is a private joke for Sally and Chris. They tease back and forth. Sometimes Chris will gaze at Sally naked and joke, "I'm looking at it." Sally will quickly come back with, "Let me know if you see anything happening."

She lies back on her pillow and marvels how ridiculously easy it is to awaken her husband's penis. "If only it were that easy for me," she thinks to herself. Sally explains to the group about how she was learning to tell Chris what aroused her and this led the group to the general discussion of intimacy and romance. Does intimacy and romance lead to arousal? Are they necessary for arousal?

Sally says that the key for her is feeling close, letting Chris in. She tells him that she wants to be held, just have his arms around her for a while. She also tells him that it's not going to happen if there is tension between them, some unresolved issue, even if it's minor such as when he was supposed to call the plumber. For her, this is more important than how or where he touches her. Once she becomes aroused, all sorts of touching by either or both of them add to it.

Sarah confessed that she wasn't sure she had ever been sexually aroused. She stated she had sex to "keep her boyfriend." Brittany says that she reads Cosmo in hopes of finding the "right position," by which she means the position that is least uncomfortable, not necessarily a position that she would find pleasurable. But, what Brittany finds in Cosmo instead is more advice about how to turn on and satisfy the guy.

Many women are faced daily with how ridiculously easy it is for their partners to become sexually aroused, while how evasive the feeling of arousal is for them. Sexually satisfying their partners can become more of a chore or a scheduled event than a pleasure. It all begins with knowing when you are sexually aroused and how to intensify it.

Women remember being a virgin as a big deal. We treasure it, are proud of it, and protect it. Once women "lose" their virginity some of them begin to devalue their sexual self, indeed their self.

> Sarah told the group, "Since I'm not a virgin anymore, having sex isn't that big of a deal, I might as well have sex with the next guy I date." Women can begin basing their sexual response on the desire of their partner instead of their own sexual arousal and desire for sexual contact. Rachel chides the group, "I have sex when I want to, when I feel like it, not when my partner wants it."

Often women we talk to find out they are sexually aroused more often than they think. Once they start paying attention to their bodies they become aware of many moments during the day when their thoughts turn sexual. They may notice an attractive person at the store or a sexy magazine ad and their bodies respond. The problem is those moments are usually not enjoyed as the busyness of their lives take over their thoughts and the experience is not noticed or savored.

Taking the time to notice when you are sexually aroused not only will make you feel more in touch with your femininity but also can improve your enjoyment of sexual activity.

Inconvenient Arousal

> Sarah had been quiet during the discussion of the women complaining about not being aroused. She stated she had a completely different problem. She had dumped her boyfriend but tells the group that whenever she runs into him at school, she still feels a warm rush "down there." She asks the group, "Does that mean I still love him?"
>
> Immediately Sally pipes in, "When you see him, do you have the open chest sensation we talked about a few sessions ago?" Sarah laughs and looks down, "No open chest anywhere in this body." The ladies all get a laugh but are then stuck in trying to figure out what Sarah should do when she feels aroused but no longer wants to have sex with her former boyfriend.

Sarah thinks the issue will take care of itself when she gets into another relationship. Rachel challenges her to do something herself and not wait for another boy to come along. Brittany says maybe it would be fun just to enjoy the feeling of arousal without any pressure to have sex.

Brittany has a similar problem. She tells the group about a cute guy in the next cubicle who flirts with her. At first she enjoyed flirting back, but then she realized she was becoming uncomfortable and concerned about her husband finding out. So for awhile she tried spurning his flirtations, acting annoyed with him. She seeks the advice of the group. Sarah says, "Why not go for it?" Sally says, "You don't want to cheat on your husband do you?" Rachel says, "Why not just go for a drink and see what happens?" This began the debate between the women on what to do when they felt aroused but didn't want to "do" anything about it.

As the women continued their discussion they decided that an important fact when paying attention to their feelings was to understand that the feeling of sexual arousal does not always mean love. To notice if they felt love they would have to check for the expansiveness in the chest area. They also focused on the difference between being aroused and wanting to act on that feeling.

If either party doesn't want to engage in sexual activity, they should respect that. Women fake orgasm frequently to make men "get off" so they will get off of them. Married women have sex all the time when they are not "into it" but would still say they are "willful" participants. Is it ok to have intimate contact when you are not aroused, or worse, turned off, disgusted, or frightened? At it's worst, it is rape and a crime.

Sarah begins to cry and tells the group about a bad experience she had had when she was fourteen. An older boy at school sat beside her on the bus and groped her. She went totally stiff but didn't say anything and kept it a secret until now.

This led to a discussion about unwanted sex, what constituted rape and what did not. The women in the group made several additional distinctions:

You don't want it and the other person is forcing himself or herself on you. You have made it clear you don't want sex and your partner forces himself or herself on you anyway. You don't want it but tolerate it because you are afraid.

The discussion among the women on lack of arousal, unwanted arousal, and rape, was lively. The women agreed that sexual arousal was an important topic for women to explore.

Regardless of whether you want to increase or decrease the sensation of sexual arousal, there is one critical point to hold onto. Women often give away their sexuality to attract a partner, to satisfy someone else's desire or to fulfill a marital requirement. Women often do not check in with their own bodies, look for their own desire or decide what they want. Our number one solution for sexual arousal is OWN IT.

Actions to Take

1. Don't have sex if you don't want to.

2. Pay attention to what stimulates your sexual arousal and what douses it.

3. Fantasize about situations, relationships, actions, and dreams to see if they arouse you (or not).

4. Know your sexual response cycle and the time of month, time of day, and type of environment that peaks your arousal.

5. Pace yourself. If you are aroused but don't want to act on that arousal, don't move into a danger zone where you may be impulsive.

6. If you think you are getting too aroused, construct barriers such as meeting in public places.

7. If you think you are not aroused enough, remove barriers. Ask him to dance. Ask for a massage.

8. Tell your partner what you want. Remember, sometimes you don't want to be more aroused, you want to be quieter, calmer but still cared about. Maybe your partner doesn't like giving back rubs, but would enjoy "mutual foot rubs." Your partner may think sexual arousal is only about intercourse, but could learn to love gentler contact.

9. If a traumatic event impacts your ability to feel sexual arousal or enjoy the feeling of sexual arousal, consider seeking help from a qualified medical or mental health professional.

Practice

Scan your groin for any hint of the feeling of tingling or warmth. Keep scanning periodically throughout the day.

Describe the situation(s) that triggers the sensation of warmth or tingling in your groin:

_____

_____

_____

Brainstorm possible solutions. Think about ways you can either increase or decrease your arousal. Be creative. If you know turning down sexual contact will be hard for you, know what you will say ahead of time when the situation presents itself. On the other hand, if you want to increase arousal, consider possible intensifiers.

_____

_____

_____

Choose a solution or combination of solutions and create a plan of ACTION.

_____

_____

_____

Review the outcome. What happened? Were you able to modulate your level of arousal? What went well? Would you do anything differently?

_____

_____

_____

OVERWHELMED

By now there are times when you are easily able to tell if you are feeling sad, angry, happy or afraid. But other times you might feel as if you are experiencing every feeling at once. The experience of feeling everything at once is being overwhelmed. It is like being on the verge of trembling, or feeling like you want to curl up and hide, feeling out of control or completely shut down. Overwhelmed is when you feel if you open your mouth all the wrong things will spill out. There is a helpless quality to this experience.

So what should you do when you are feeling overwhelmed?

All four of the women voiced frequent experiences with being overwhelmed, saying that typically they would just "suffer quietly" and try not to show it.

Rachel said that sometimes she would "fight back" and get into an argument, and that this typically resulted in feeling even more overwhelmed.

The workshop guidelines, described in this book, lay out a simple rule for what to do when you are overwhelmed: You must leave the situation. That's right, YOU MUST LEAVE THAT SITUATION IMMEDIATELY!

We don't mean permanently move to another country, throw up your hands, and never address important issues. We recommend that you leave the situation when you feel overwhelmed and return to the situation after you have had time to calm down and are no longer feeling overwhelmed.

How long it takes you to calm down when you are feeling overwhelmed depends in part on how urgent your situation is and partly on what you do with yourself while you try to calm down. Rehearsing catastrophic or negative thoughts will keep you spun up. Calming down looks more like creating space to gain physical calm and mental clarity.

Leaving the situation when you are overwhelmed allows you to accomplish both of these important goals and maybe more importantly, prevents you from escalating the situation. Deescalating is as simple and urgent as that.

"Leave the situation" may mean to pull off the road and stop in a safe place, it may mean to leave a room and sit quietly in another room, to leave a house and visit a friend or sit in a park or a library. This response focuses on the next few minutes or perhaps an hour, that's all. But you must do it.

Creating even a few moments of solitude by sitting alone in the bathroom, taking a shower or going for a run can do wonders for returning your body to a calm state. If someone's physical safety is in jeopardy, consider calling on someone else to stand in for you to watch or protect your children, an ailing partner, or elder adult. The point is that once you are no longer overwhelmed you will be in a better place to think about solutions for the underlying problem. But while you are overwhelmed you are in no condition to do so. The good news is that, as you get better at noticing your body sensations you will reduce the frequency of feeling overwhelmed. You will be taking care of issues before they get to the "overwhelm" state.

Actions to Take

1. Leave the situation. Create a space to be alone and calm yourself mentally and physically.

2. Calm yourself while you are alone. Stop thoughts that are inflaming. Refuse to think on self-defeating ideas or thoughts of helplessness.

3. Breathe deeply.

4. Tighten and relax your muscles. Start in your feet and work your way up your body.

5. If someone's physical safety could be in jeopardy, consider calling on someone else to stand in for you to watch or protect your children, an ailing partner, or elder adult.

Practice

Scan your body for any hint of feeling overwhelmed. Keep scanning periodically throughout the day.

Describe the situation(s) that triggers the sensation of being overwhelmed:

_____

_____

_____

Brainstorm possible solutions. Think about ways you can calm down. Be creative.

_____

_____

_____

Choose a solution or combination of solutions and create a plan of ACTION.

_____

_____

_____

Review the outcome. What happened? Where you able to calm down? What went well? Would you do anything differently?

_____

_____

_____

HYBRID FEELINGS

Sometimes you will be aware that you are having more than one body sense at the same time.

> *Sally sat on the edge of her bed staring at her phone ringing. This was the third time her mother had called her this week and Sally was painfully aware of the tension between her shoulder blades as she looked at the phone. However, Sally also was aware of a slightly racy feeling in her gut and didn't know what to make of this mingling of*

feeling. She knew she was annoyed at having her mother call so often but what was the feeling of fear about?

Instead of answering the telephone, Sally grabbed her Journal and started going through the problem-solving steps. Tension was the most intense feeling and so she started with it and easily jotted down awareness of being interrupted by her mother's frequent calls as the trigger for feeling tension between her shoulder blades. Next she brainstormed several ways of resolving the tension, like not answering the phone, turning off the ringer, asking her mother to call less often, making an excuse why she couldn't talk and telling her mother that she was calling too much.

Next, Sally broke down the racy feeling and sat for a moment trying to figure out the trigger for this feeling. Sally noticed that hearing the telephone ringing and seeing her mother on Caller ID resulted in Sally wondering what was wrong. Thoughts of her mother being in trouble, being sick or needing help tumbled out.

Sally brainstormed solutions to resolve the racy feeling and came up with getting a caretaker or a weekly nurse to check in on her mother, to get her mother's neighbors to check on her regularly, and to talk with her mother about Sally's concerns and her mother's possible health needs.

Sally glanced over both of her brainstorming lists and noticed what would resolve one feeling might only intensify the other. If Sally chose not to answer the phone to resolve the feeling of tension the racy feeling might intensify because she would worry if her mother was OK. Sally was tempted to give up. Her workshop group reminded her that her body's feelings were there to give her direction on what to do with everyday situations just like this one.

Sally closed her eyes and continued to brainstorm. "What if there was a way to set a limit with her mother and not worry about her?" Inspiration evaded her and she decided to simply share what she was feeling with her mother and try brainstorming together. The next time her mother called, Sally scanned her body for sensation and again felt tension and racy. She answered the telephone and calmly stated, "Mom, I notice you are calling more the last few weeks. Sometimes the phone ringing interrupts me but I worry that if I don't answer it you might need me. I'm not sure what to do about this and wanted to get your ideas of how we can work together."

Sally's mother sounded a bit defensive, "I'm not in any trouble, I just want to check in with you." Sally's racy feeling disappeared almost immediately, but the tension between her shoulder blades was becoming more intense. Sally knew it was time to set a limit. "Mom, how about you check in with me once a week if you just want to chat and any other time if you need something?"

The silence that followed made Sally wonder if she had done the right thing but she said nothing and gave her mom time to gather her thoughts. "Whatever you like," was all her mother said and then quickly hung up.

Sally's first thought was that she should have just kept her mouth shut but then immediately reflected on how unproductive that would have been. What if her mother's calls became even more frequent? Sally also reminded herself that she was new to setting limits with her mother and maybe they both would need some time to get used to the new style. She made a firm commitment to keep listening to her body and using that wisdom to increase the satisfaction in her relationship with her mom.

At the next workshop session Sally reported that days had past with no calls from her mom. Instead of telling herself she was a bad daughter, Sally praised herself for listening to her body and doing something about what she was feeling. If she starting hearing conflicting ideas in her head, Sally would simply tell herself, "This takes time. I'll figure it out as I go along."

On Tuesday, seven days to the date of their last conversation, her telephone rang and Sally noticed no tension, just a slight racy feeling. She easily figured the racy feeling was being scared her mother would be upset with her. Sally answered the phone and immediately told her mother she was wondering how her mother was doing. The conversation was short and lacked some of the warmth but she kept track of her body sensations and quickly realized her racy feeling had disappeared and no tension was present during or immediately after the call. Sally praised herself for sticking to her plan.

Over the next few weeks, the conversations between Sally and her mother remained at one time per week. Sally noticed that she would miss talking to her mother if it had been eight days since their last call and would pick up the phone herself to call her mom. Their conversations also became longer in length and the two began talking *about the demands in Sally's life and the surplus of time Sally's mom had. Sally encouraged her mother to join a hobby group and her mom recommended Sally spend less time texting and more time sleeping. The two would usually laugh at this point. These weekly telephone calls became something both women looked forward to and a time to connect and share with each other.*

Learning how to manage feeling blends rests on your ability to distinguish and identify each feeling separately. If you are still finding it difficult to localize and describe internal sensations or feelings, don't give up. Practice! Get curious about what your body is telling you and allow yourself to describe these sensations in your own words.

Actions to Take

1. Name each feeling you are experiencing by localizing it in your body and describing the sensation. Start with the most intense or dominant feeling.

2. For each separate feeling, identify the specific situation that triggered that sensation.

3. Beginning with the dominant feeling, the sensation that is the most intense, brainstorm possible solutions to resolve the feeling.

4. Continue brainstorming possible solutions to resolve each feeling in order of intensity, from most intense to least intense.

5. Choose a solution or combination of solutions to address resolving the dominant feeling and if possible the additional less dominant sensation(s).

6. Act.

7. Notice whether the intensity of the dominant feeling increased or decreased and whether the intensity of the less intense feelings increased or decreased.

8. Repeat these steps if a dominant feeling remains or if the blend remains.

Practice

Scan your body for any hint of feeling more than one feeling at once. Keep scanning periodically throughout the day.

Describe the situation(s) that triggers more than one feeling in your body at the same time:

_____

_____

_____

Take the more intense sensation and brainstorm possible solutions. Think about ways you can resolve this feeling. Be creative.

_____

_____

_____

Take the less intense sensation and brainstorm possible solutions. Think about ways you can resolve this feeling. Be creative.

_____

_____

_____

Choose a solution or combination of solutions and create a plan of ACTION to address BOTH feelings.

_____

_____

_____

Review the outcome. What happened? Where you able to resolve the dominant feeling and/or the less intense feeling? What went well? Would you do anything differently?

_____

_____

_____

GENERAL SOLUTIONS FOR FEELINGS

There may be a time when you are at a loss for what to do with what you are feeling or may even be in the dark about what you are feeling. Do not despair! This section will offer you some general solutions to feelings.

Think of these guidelines as general principles to use to manage feelings. Turn to this section of the book when you do not know what else to do and need some direction. Return to this section of the book six weeks after finishing reading of this book and periodically thereafter to review your progress and make sure you are using the skills you have learned.

Here are some general pointers to help you manage most of your feelings.

1. First and most importantly, always pay attention to those signals from inside your body, those internal sensations.

2. Pay attention to when the feeling begins; don't wait until the feeling is intense or painful.

3. See if you can notice the initial trigger for the feeling when it starts. That's often the best cue to what's happening.

4. In general, do something immediately. Brainstorm solutions and act.

5. If you are at a loss for something to say, try something simple like "Gee I'm feeling tense for some reason." or "Hmm, I'm feeling a bit nervous right now."

6. If the feeling has changed or is getting even stronger, whatever you are doing isn't working, try something else.

7. Be realistic. Life is not as depicted on television or the movies. Many situations take time to work through and multiple strategies to resolve. Pay attention to your body, think, act and review your progress so you can make adjustments as needed.

8. Don't guess what you are feeling, for example, it is easy to confuse anger with fear and fear with anger. Feel your body and let your body give you the true answer.

MOVING FORWARD

This book has explained how to use your body to know what you are feeling. When you know what you feel, you are able to act in consistent ways to either intensify or resolve what you feel.

Women progress in knowing their body senses at different paces. Some women are intrinsically hooked into their internal sensations. For other women, even remembering to pay attention to their internal sensations takes much effort.

When paying attention to your body sensations becomes second nature, you will discover that you are able to recognize the causes of your feelings when they first arise and can prevent situations from escalating. You will feel grounded and confident. Others will see you as more down-to-earth, steadier. You will enjoy the pleasant sensations of happiness and love more intensely and resolve the troubling sensations of fear, anger, sadness, and longing more quickly.

We look forward to staying in touch with you. Tune into our podcasts and come join us at our workshops.

GLOSSARY

Anger

The internal sensation of tension between the shoulder blades that spreads to the neck, jaw and face and even into the hands. An emotion associated with being trespassed against that sometimes leads to aggressive thought and behavior.

Bladder Pressure

Internal sensation of pressure in the bladder that is universally recognized as associated with the need to urinate.

Body Sense

An internal sensation associated with a feeling or emotion. The sensation is localized to a specific area in the body and fluctuates over time from absent, to barely noticeable, to intense, to painful.

Disgust

The sensation of gagging in the throat that is accompanied by a feeling of repulsion that leads to avoidance of the stimulus.

Embarrassment

The sensation of flushing or warming of the face and a feeling of self-consciousness that occurs in a situation of social exposure or vulnerability.

Emotion

A biological state evolved for the survival or well-being of the species, society, and/or the self. An emotion typically has three components, a physiological state which can be experienced as a feeling or body sensation, a behavior state consisting of facial expressions or predisposition to actions evolved to respond for survival, and thoughts about the meaning of the state. Traditionally the term emotion has been applied to the following: anger, fear, sadness, and happiness.

Feelings

A term used as a synonym for emotion, or a synonym for sensations in our body, or for intuitions that are more accurately identified as thoughts or beliefs.

Happiness

The sensation of an open light feeling across the chest that occurs during positive events and that is experienced as pleasurable.

Heartache

The sensation of an aching pressure or weightiness in the middle of the chest that is associated with separation or an inability to connect with a loved one or something wanted or desired.

Hybrid Feelings

The experience of more than one feeling at the same moment in time.

Internal Sensations

Sensations that arise from within the body as opposed to sensations which arise from the skin, eyes or ears. Examples include, but are not limited to, bladder pressure, bowel cramps, hunger, sadness, fear, and anger.

Intimacy

There are three types of intimacy; intellectual, emotional and physical. Intellectual intimacy is the sharing of beliefs, convictions, and aspirations. Emotional intimacy is the sharing of feelings. Physical intimacy is the sharing of bodies.

Irritability

The sensation of tension between the shoulder blades and edginess that corresponds with thoughts of intolerance and impatient or rude behavior.

Longing

See 'heartache'

Loving

The sensation of an open light feeling across the chest and a feeling of closeness with another person or beloved object. It is typically associated with thoughts and behavior intended to help and care for the other.

Sadness

The sensation of a lump in the throat or moisture in the eyes that is associated with thoughts of loss and behavior such as crying or sobbing which elicits sympathy in others.

Sensation

A sensation is a direct experience of something seen, heard, or felt. Felt sensations can be on the skin or inside the body.

Sexual Activity

Genital or other intimate contact or exposure with the intent to sexually arouse.

Sexual Arousal

The sensation of warm tingling in the groin that spreads up into the belly associated with thoughts of desire for sexual activity.

Stress

A general term for events or memories that cause distress, and if prolonged can adversely affect one's health.

BIOGRAPHIES

Heidi A. Sauder, Ph.D., received her doctorate of philosophy in clinical psychology with advanced studies and research investigating the role of emotions and physiological response in human interaction. Dr. Sauder currently works in private practice in Lone Tree, Colorado and can be contacted through her website at www.sauderpsychology.com.

Dr. David R. Hubbard is a board-certified neurologist who spent the early part of his career in pain management and drug development for muscle pain. He has had a life-long interest in the mind-brain problem, majored in philosophy at Yale, receiving a Masters in Counseling Psychology at Stanford, an MD at University of Connecticut and his neurology training at Albert Einstein College of Medicine where he was chief resident. He is Medical Director of the Applied fMRI Institute in San Diego. You may visit his website at www.appliedfmri.com.

Leanna R. Fredrich is a Denver-based, nationally recognized, Career Coach, Life Coach, Trainer, Workshop Facilitator, Author, and Infopreneur. You may visit her website at www.AmazingMondays.com